# REMISSION
# PURIFICATION POEMS

BY DAVID E. DOWD

WestBow Press books may be ordered through booksellers or by contacting:

WestBow Press
A Division of Thomas Nelson & Zondervan
1663 Liberty Drive
Bloomington, IN 47403
www.westbowpress.com
844-714-3454

Interior Image Credit: Mr Erik L. Wake

ISBN: 979-8-3850-0799-8 (sc)
ISBN: 979-8-3850-0800-1 (e)

Library of Congress Control Number: 2023917640

Print information available on the last page.

WestBow Press rev. date: 1/31/2024

WESTBOW
PRESS°
A DIVISION OF THOMAS NELSON
& ZONDERVAN

BASED ON THE RETREAT @ ST BENEDICT ABBEY
GIVEN BY FATHER JAMES BUCKLEY FSSP
ON

THE SPIRITUAL EXERCISES OF ST. IGNATIUS

# Table of Contents

# INSPIRATION

## PRAISE, REVERENCE AND SERVE

PURIFICATION POEMS
BASED ON RETREAT
INSPIRED BY ART
IN THE OUR LADY OF GUADALUPE CHAPEL
ST BENEDICT ABBEY
STILL RIVER, MA.
07-28/31-2011

## BY THIS MEANS SAVE YOUR SOUL

AND SO
A POET SERVES
TO INSPIRE ATTENDANCE
AT RETREATS
BASED ON THE SPIRITUAL EXERCISES
OF ST. IGNATIUS

# BEING INDIFFERENT

10:54 AM 072911

Each sunrise, ask yourself as light streams in:
Give praise, in prayer, below life's noisy din.
Seek ye reverence to Him in Sacraments.
Please, can you serve, in joy, the folks He sent?

Recall creation's there to save your soul.
Hence, make use, all things to help you reach this goal.
But, rid ye fast, if hindrance prove to be.
Indifferent then, if pleasures doth deceive.

If sickness, poverty, or a short life,
Or even if dishonor, and, or, if, strife
Are the path of thorns to your salvation,
Or, If health and wealth take fast vacation,
Peer through worldly challenges to see your end.
(Pray) Will your heart open to love He sends?

# INDIFFERENCE

1:58 PM 072911

And so, we practice creature indifference.
In soul movements, we study for inference.
In deep ocean currents, learn to discern.
From good and bad spirits, so much to learn.

Harmonies felt, when steeped in mortal sin,
Are stung when good spirits rouse hope again.
Desolation thoughts may disturb the soul.
Unleashed by evil spirits' wicked goal.

Resist with God's help, remain firm in prayer.
Do the opposite, fast. Don't take the dare.
Go counter to the devil's suggestion.
Offering penance, just makes him question.
"Interior joy will return", Keep Faith!
"In sweet consolation!" angels' saith.

# PURIFICATION AND THE HUNTER

4:37 PM 072911

Fallen though we are, we ask God for grace.
Reflect inside imagination's space.
Memory, intellect, and will are three
Powers of the soul to set us free.

We creatures bow before our Creator.
Corruptible bodies' sinful equator.
Cannot make progress unless purged of sin.
And if no sanctifying grace is the state we're in.

Consider each mortal sin has effect.
Through an angel's fall, salvation is wrecked.
He's wily, deceitful and wants your soul!
Kill, steal and destroy is his wicked goal.
So probe with your intellect: Spark your will!
Purify your soul: sin's effect, do kill!

# SPEED DEMONS

4:46 PM 072911

Angels created in the state of grace:
Greater in spirit then the human race.
Some did not use their freedom to reverence God.
The Fallen bite in temptation's gnaws.

They sought higher places than they deserved.
"Non-serviam" motto led them to swerve.
Grace turns to hatred through their fall in pride.
Fast fall from heaven: misery's ride.

# SECOND EXERCISE
# GOD'S SURPRISE

10:15 PM 072911

Ask in growing, intense sorrow.
Provokes movement of your will. Tomorrow or today!
If loathsomeness and malice
From dualism's interior palace

Seem to separate the body and the soul.
Committing mortal sin doth take a toll.
Humble yourself! Who is this tiny man?
In all mankind? Less than a speck of sand.

Know! Corruption and contagion spread fast,
Infecting souls with damages that last.
Compared to God's true love, my weakness fans!
I whiff! While men, of good heart, fill the stands.
Believe! Angels and saints answer begging prayers.
Unmoved, our Lord provokes when He cares.

# "SERVIAM" OR "NON-SERVIAM" THAT IS THE QUESTION!

6:45 AM 073011

Sin separates us from the love of God.
Cannot love or serve He who we do not laud.
Sorrow for sin; interior penance
In eating and sleep, practice ye temperance.

Keep in mind, "I am sorry", feel pain
Permit not your thoughts to run random like rain.
You've offended the Lord who gives you gifts.
The prisoner, you are, caused so many rifts.

Stand for the moment of an Our Father.
In His great love, know He does bother!
He loves you despite your wretched, poor sins.
(Priests hear confession) **** Forgiving is in! ****
Spend time in reflection. But if you fail,
His grace is transcendent. You don't remain in jail!

# THOUGHTS FROM
# THE IMITATION OF CHRIST

8:50 AM 073011

Did you hear Thomas a Kempis, heretofore?
Imitate Christ, acknowledge Him more.
Consider Hell's punishment for our sins.
Then consider the state your soul is in!

Hunger is torture for a glutton.
Imagine you're starving. Not even mutton!
If in your life, you just sought vainglory,
Hell is full of those who hate your story!

Think of your attachments. You can lose, by them.
Just one mortal sin? You've a BIG problem!
Grace for your salvation disappears.
Find God's peace in the source of your fears.
For, trees rooted in shifting sands, fall and die.
Your soul to save! In this life, try!

# EXAMEN ON LUST

9:02 PM 073011

Imagine a canvas, you're a painter.
What could you draw? If you're growing fainter?
Try this for size, hold on to your brush.
Paint your mortal sins, be not in a rush.

Be fearless and bold, each one is a knife.
Destroy's your soul's grace, creates external strife.
Don't know what they are? You better learn fast!
Or suffer forever as eternal trash.

Sin's not old fashioned, don't listen to those
Who seek after pleasure as their life's goals.
Satan allures us in pleasure's fine threads.
Intensely arousing us, even in our beds.
All procreation, Satan wipes from our mind.
Wounding our souls, catching us in his bind!

9

# FOR ETERNAL LIFE: SMOKING OR NON SMOKING?

11:05 AM 073011

For the grace of final perseverance,
I, now, beg. Consider the appearance
Of a prosecuting attorney at
Your final judgement. Imagine you sat,

While a demon reads your baptismal vows.
Accusing with malice, breaking down how
You ignored God's commandments every time you sinned.
Can you hear his laugh from the coffin you're in?

St. Basil says, "Then your conscience appears!"
But more painful are the next words you hear.
Soon, in a voice, you will never forget,
When your eyes and Jesus' sad eyes met,
"What more could I have done," He asks of you.
One Mortal Sin? Eternal flames are your due!

# BEGINNINGS

1:29 PM 073011

And then one fine day, you stop and you ask,
What He did for you gives you a new task.
Love is giving and love is receiving.
Your time has come to start believing!

What have I done? What will I do?
For the One who is so thoroughly true!
And so a general examination,
Now, has serious ramification!

You finally see your life steeped in sin.
And feel the shame you gathered within.

Where do you start, you don't want to wallow.
You decide, "particular" follows.
You record In your notebook with a good pen.
Mark the number of times you fall in your sin!
If anger toward self or your fellow man,
Charity says, "Start here with your plan".

Bad language can change from 30 times a day.
Progress follows when you watch what you say.
Up til now you thought nothing about this,
You'd slip into vice but felt no remiss.

Now, you touch your heart with each new mistake.
The progress you make could change your own fate.
Each touch on your heart is marked on your pad.
(Your kids might discover a more loveable dad!)

You're not restricted. Eliminate faults.
The deeper you dig, you find deeper vaults.
But virtue unleashed is like summer breeze.
When each fresh wind blows, virtue calms stormy seas..

But your work on your faults doesn't stop there.
Said the priest whose insight revealed God's care,
Like cultivating a flower garden,
Acquire virtue like Father Hardon.

There is ALWAYS room for growth in your heart.
To acquire patience: Just make a new start.
Can you be more humble? You can try.
Acquire these virtues before you die!

If you bring grief to those where you work.
If your co-workers say you're a jerk.
Though sin may be venial, here you can start.
To pray for the grace to have a strong heart.

Be mindful, each time, your words bring complaint.
Respect good intentions, good people don't taint.
Guard carefully against your sin or defect.
Correct and improve. You feel self-respect.

Ask God for grace. Know, you have fallen.
Renew resolution. Salvation is calling!
Examine your conscience two times a day.
Spiritual life strengthens each time you pray!

# FIFTH EXERCISE:
# MEDITATION ON HELL

4:02 PM 073011

Praise, Reverence, Serve man as created.
Remember, some appetites are never sated.
And so St. Ignatius reminds us of Hell.
Imagine to this wicked place is where you fell!

Exiled in vile body among brute beasts.
Pains of loss and sense are ours, for sinful feats.
"We are forever in heaven or forever in hell."
(St. Francis of Assisi tried to tell)

"Out of my sight into everlasting flame."
Christ said in St Matthew. (*this ain't no game!*)
In pain of sense, we hear wailing and howling.
And scents smell worse then burned buildings fouling.

No escaping the torture of the damned.
No matter if you're loved by Uncle Sam.
Or even if you're a home town hero.
With one mortal sin, you're a big fat zero.
Hell lasts forever. Reached by deception and lies.
No more of God's grace, no last college try.

# AND SO YOU EXAMEN

7:45 PM 073011

Find an old examen, see what the saints meant.
Begin your examen on God's own commandments.
Remember to confess sins of the tongue.
Blasphemy, swearing, detraction are some.

Mortal and deadly sins, broken Church laws.
Here, sins against virtue find their grave cause.
But, merit is gained, so resist evil thoughts.
Conquering these. Lifelong, brave mission sought.

If pleasures allow vice even for brief times.
Your will can weaken, evil is that sublime.
So pay no heed if a siren doth call.
So you won't be set up for a sinful fall.
Pray. Then list your sins before you confess.
Challenge yourself to pass rigorous test.

# PRAYER BEFORE AND AFTER COMMUNION

9:50 PM 073011

What dispositions are required for Daily Communion?
Whose graces are stored for Spiritual union?
Did spiritual exercises prepare in proportion?
Do recipients care?

Now to be taken for serious prayer!
Practice these precepts. (They should not be rare)
You'll be more recollected when you receive.
And, in greater happiness then you could conceive!

Please wash away filth, plead your contrition.
Doctor Aquinas' humble petition.
Seeking Eucharistic graces as your goal.
(Might just induce salvation in your soul)

After Communion, thanksgiving is due.
Prayer of St. Bonaventure is just and true:
"If Thou spare us, we correct not our ways."
Seek God's compassion revealed, read what He says!
Xavier's "But as Thyself, thou has loved me." Verse
Reveals in our trials, we see God's love traverse!

# JOHN 6

9:01 AM 073111

Seeing the multitudes gathered on the hill.
Jesus prepared their eternal spiritual fill.
From five barley loaves and two little fish,
Now, Jesus prepared a miracle dish!

There, He prefigured Eucharist's meal.
For, on Him, God, the Father, set His seal!
"Do whatever He tells you," Mary said.
Jesus blessed the five thousand, He then fed.

But still Jews murmured and questioned Him
(He also walked on water! Did not swim!)
(And, He said), "He who eats Me will live because of Me."
(We believe our sense of hearing.), said He.
He gave His Flesh to eat and Blood to drink.
Eternal Living Bread! Stop and Think!

# ONLY SIN

9:10 07 31 11

All sacraments transmit, to us, graces
Christ won for us on Calvary. In our faces,
See the windows to our souls. If there,
Reflect, substance of eternal worth, so rare,

Assimilate more like Christ in me! The Host.
Love. Father, Son and Holy Ghost.
His Body, Blood, Divinity and Soul.
Only Sin.... Prevents meeting this goal.